Running ACROSS America

A True Story
of Dreams, Determination,
and Heading for Home

Dave McGillivray
Boston Marathon Race Director

with Nancy Feehrer
Illustrated by Shululu

Dedication

This book is dedicated to the important work done by Dana-Farber Cancer Institute and its Jimmy Fund (jimmyfund.org) and to all the children and adults who are bravely battling cancer—and yet still running for their dreams!

And to The Joseph Middlemiss Big Heart Foundation (jmbigheart.org) for their inspiring, life-changing mission to promote kindness in honor of heart-warriors Joseph and Jack Middlemiss.

We are thankful, too, for the gift of Grace!

A portion of the proceeds from the sale of this book will be donated to these charities.

Acknowledgments

The authors would like to thank: Alex and Susan Kahan from Nomad Press for their enthusiastic support; our invaluable readers for their thoughtful suggestions; the original RV Crew: Dan Carey, Jeff Donohoe, Kent Hawley, Tom Kinder; and our encouraging, patient families: Katie, Ryan, Max, Elle, Luke, and Chloe McGillivray; and John, Derek, Nate, Tim, and Izzie Feehrer

Nomad Press
A division of Nomad Communications
10 9 8 7 6 5 4 3 2 1
Copyright © 2019 by DMSE Foundation, Inc. All rights reserved.

This book was manufactured by CGB Printers,
North Mankato, Minnesota, United States
September 2019, Job #280797

ISBN: 978-1-61930-875-6

Questions regarding the ordering of this book should be addressed to

Nomad Press
2456 Christian St.
White River Junction, VT 05001

www.nomadpress.net

Printed in the United States.

A voice booms over the
baseball park loudspeaker.

"It's going . . . going . . . **GONE!**

A home run by Daaaaave McGillivray!"

Thousands of Red Sox fans jump to their feet cheering
as I round third base and head for home.

"Dave!
            Dave!
                    Dave!"

"Dave! Dave!"
Mom shouts out the back door. "It's dinnertime!"
My older brother laughs and shakes his head.
"He's just dreaming about hitting a home run—**again**."

I never did become a professional baseball player,
but I did become a runner.
When I was 19, I heard about someone biking
3,000 miles across America.

**"What a great idea!" I thought.
"But instead of a bike, I'll use my sneakers!"**

For four years, I planned a cross-country run from Medford,
Oregon, to my hometown of Medford, Massachusetts.

One night, I left all my research out for my parents to see.
Would they try to talk me out of it?

Later, I went back into the kitchen.
On one of the binders was a note.
"David, we love you."

That was all the encouragement I needed!

Run for your dreams.

Since I'm a Red Sox fan, I called their charity,
the Jimmy Fund, to ask if I could do this run
to raise money for children's cancer research.

Their answer came fast: YES!

Together, we came up with a plan:
I would start at a Red Sox game on the West Coast
and finish 80 days later at a Red Sox game on the East Coast.

Home would be the magnet pulling me back.

The night before I left,
my family threw a huge goodbye party for me.
But I felt doubt creep in around the joy.

Can I do this? What if I fail?

Fear and panic followed me onto the airplane.
They flew with me as I looked down at the country
that I now had to run back across.

What was I thinking?

BIG dreams require BIG faith.

The announcer's voice echoed across the Kingdome.

"This evening, a 23-year-old marathon runner is going to embark on quite a mission. He is going to run coast to coast . . ."

Sweat poured down my face.
I didn't wait for the announcer to finish!
I ran into the stadium. The crowd stood up and clapped.

". . . and if all goes as scheduled,
he will end at Fenway Park in 80 days.
We wish him the best."

"IF all goes as scheduled," I thought,
as I rounded third base.

All I wanted to do now was head for home.

When in doubt, keep running.

June 11, 1978: Day One

In Medford, Oregon, friends were waiting for me in an RV.
It would be our home away from home for the next three months.
TV crews and newspaper reporters were there to see me off.
The mayor even ran with me for the first few miles.

Was I ready to run 40 miles, every day, for 80 days straight?

I'd soon find out.

I got into a good routine right away:
    wake up at 5:30 and stretch,
        eat some toast with honey,
           run 10 miles,
              then rest for 20 minutes.

I repeated this ALL day, stopping only for lunch and a nap. When it was dinnertime, I marked my stopping point with a sweaty old T-shirt, where I would start again the next day.

What surprised me in California?

The spectacular Sierra Mountains, how cold it was, how sore I was (*already*), and that sometimes, people would take my sweaty old T-shirts!!

Good routines are good for you.

In Nevada, the heat soared!
I threw water on my head to try to stay cool.

In the evenings, the rattlesnakes came out.
I could hear their buzzing, vibrating tails.

Fortunately, my friends were there to help me and keep me company. Unfortunately, my knees hurt so much from running up and down mountains that my friends had to rush me to the hospital.

Was my journey ending already?

The doctor said, "Rest!" But I had more than 2,000 miles to go!

Instead of resting, I alternated running on each side of the road.
I prayed and focused on positive things—not on the pain.

What did Nevada teach me?

Surround yourself with good people
because it's impossible to go it alone.
(Oh, and rattlesnakes improve running times.)

There is no such thing as an individual accomplishment.

Before I went to sleep each night,
I wrote postcards and letters and made notes in my journal.
Memories fade, and you can't get them back.

A thousand miles into my journey, and
I was homesick.

At the first mail stop,
I hoped for just a tiny reminder of home.

Here's what I found:

Dear Dave McGillivray

I read about you in the newspaper. Once I walked 20 miles for the March of Dimes and my feet hurt so bad. Your feet must hurt an awful lot, too. I'm proud that we have the same last name.

Robbie McGill

We raised money for kids with cancer! ♡ ♡

Tuesday   June 20. 1978

Everyone I meet is praying for you. People you don't even know...

I'm so proud to be your mother. Of course, I always was.

Dear. Dave McGillivray

To: Dave M

Kind words are fuel for the journey.

13

In Colorado, I ran through a little town named
"Dinosaur" and up a pass called "Rabbit Ears."
I even ran past "Poodle Lake."

"Are you going to run over the Rocky Mountains?"
a woman asked me.
"Yes!" I told her.
"Hmmm . . . ," she paused. "You won't make it alive."

I forced a smile, and with a confidence I didn't quite feel, I replied,

"Wait and see!"

WELCOME TO
ROCKY MOUNTAIN
NATIONAL
PARK

14

12,183 feet later,
there we were—at the top!

What did I discover in Colorado?

Don't give up when people doubt you
or even when you doubt yourself.
Wait and see—because the view
from the top is spectacular.

Every dream is sprinkled with doubts. Dream anyway!

In Nebraska, there were millions of grasshoppers.
Millions!
I ran through five straight days of grasshoppers.

Nebraska was . . . crunchy.

Almost halfway home! But then, we checked the map.

My cross-country run was not 3,250 miles, but closer to 3,450 miles. This would mean five *more* days of running!

But I didn't have more days. Instead, I'd have to add *miles* to my *days*. I started getting up earlier and earlier to make up the extra miles. One morning, I was running in the dark when I smelled a strong minty smell.

Instead of rubbing lotion on my legs that morning, I had slathered on toothpaste!

If you make a mistake, have a good laugh!

17

Running through the "vowel" states
seemed quicker than the vast western states.

But there were still hundreds of miles between me and home.

Could I finish on time? Would I finish at all?

"Remember why you're running, Dave," I told myself.
"For kids with cancer who can't run." That thought helped
during the days when I ran all 50 miles in the pouring rain.

By the time we got to Ohio, I was so sick of the rain, I stripped down to my shorts, grabbed a bar of soap, and took a shower in the downpour. People driving by thought I was nuts!

Have a "sunny" attitude, even in the pouring rain.

As I ran up and down the endless hills of Pennsylvania,
a screaming siren jolted me from my quiet run.

A state trooper was pulling me over. Me!

"If you cause a traffic accident,
I'm going to arrest you," he said in a stern voice.

"Oh . . . okay, Officer," I said, my voice shaking.

"I promise I'll be careful."

A few miles down the road, we parked the RV. A curious woman came out of her house. "What in the world are you doing?"

"Running across the United States!" I smiled.

"Running? Are you crazy?" She went back into her house. A few minutes later, she came out with chocolate ice cream! I thanked her, ice cream dripping down my chin.

Sometimes you get yelled at. Sometimes you get ice cream. Be polite either way.

Two days before my birthday, as I ran through Upstate
New York, a car drove up slowly beside me.
Was I being pulled over again?

I looked up and there was my family waving and laughing!

That night, we had a party in the RV with one big cake,
24 candles, a few presents, and

Lots of love.

"Family is not an important thing. It's everything."
—Michael J. Fox

Two days later, I crossed into Massachusetts and ran a relaxing 24 miles to celebrate my 24th birthday.

As I ran through my home state, pure joy washed over me:

I was so close to accomplishing my dream!

24

As I got closer to my hometown, I heard shouts,
sirens, cheers, and church bells.

"You did it!" "Congratulations!"
"Welcome back!"

That night, I would officially end my run across
America with a lap around Fenway Park.

Home Sweet Home.

August 29, 1978: Day 80

A voice boomed over the baseball park loudspeaker:

"Ladies and gentlemen! A Fenway Park greeting for Daaave McGillivray!"

More than 30,000 Red Sox fans jumped to their feet, cheering as I ran onto the famous field.

"Dave! Dave! Dave!"

Finally, I had a home run at Fenway!

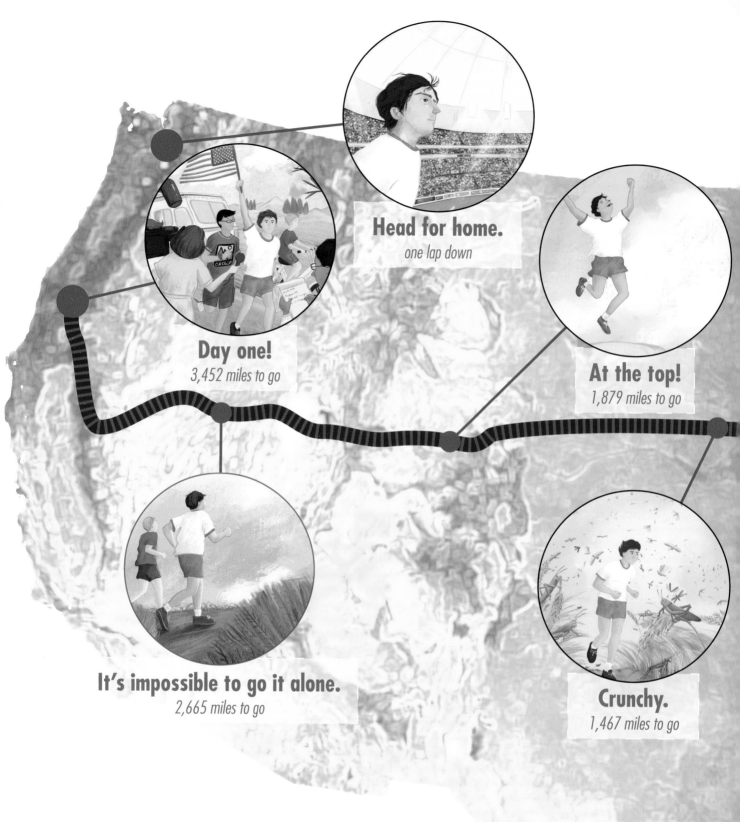

Head for home.
one lap down

Day one!
3,452 miles to go

At the top!
1,879 miles to go

It's impossible to go it alone.
2,665 miles to go

Crunchy.
1,467 miles to go

I've worked hard to accomplish many dreams.

Whenever someone asks how I got this far in life,
I grin and point to my sneakers!

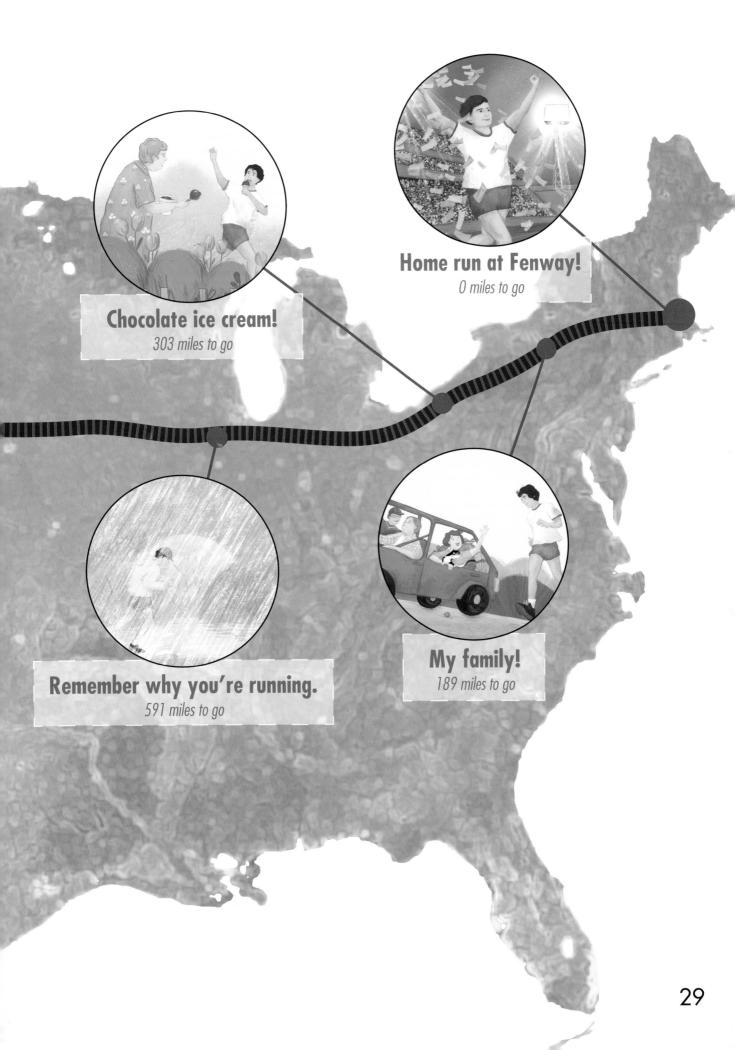

Chocolate ice cream!
303 miles to go

Home run at Fenway!
0 miles to go

Remember why you're running.
591 miles to go

My family!
189 miles to go

The DREAM BIG "Marathon"

To make your **BIG DREAMS** come true, you need to **BE FIT**—physically, mentally, and emotionally. Challenge yourself to **run** 26 miles, **read** 26 books, and **do** 26 acts of kindness in 26 weeks!

RUN! 26 MILES

Try running or walking just a mile at a time. Go to **DreamBigWithDave.org** to get started. There, you can download a printable sheet to keep track of your 26-week challenge. Check with your doctor first to make sure you're healthy and then *get moving!*

READ! 26 BOOKS

For ideas on great books for any age or interest, go to **Scholastic.com**. Just learning to read? Have an adult read to you. Reading chapter books? Aim for 10 pages a day or about 70 pages a week.

REACH OUT!
26 ACTS OF BIG-HEARTED KINDNESS

For a list of creative acts of kindness, check out The Joseph Middlemiss Big Heart Foundation at **JMBigHeart.org**. While you're there, read about Joseph's story and the amazing acts of kindness the Big Heart Foundation does.

THE FINISH LINE!

Go to **DreamBigWithDave.org** to find out how to get your very own *Dream Big "Marathon" Race Medal** for making it to the finish line!

*while supplies last.